VISIT OF SUBHAS CHANDRA BOSE TO POLAND IN JULY 1933

NEW DOCUMENTS, NEW CONCLUSIONS

Dr. Marek Moroń

KW
KNOWLEDGE WORLD

KW Publishers Pvt Ltd
New Delhi

in association with

Calcutta University
Kolkata

The Court of Directors of the East India Company sent a despatch in July, 1854 to the Governor-General of India in Council, suggesting the establishment of the Universities of Calcutta, Madras and Bombay.

In pursuance of that despatch, the University of Calcutta was founded on January 24, 1857.

The University adopted in the first instance, the pattern of the University of London and gradually introduced modifications in its constitution.

ISBN 978-93-83649-52-5

KNOWLEDGE WORLD

2011 BEST PUBLISHERS AWARD (ENGLISH)

Contents

Contents

INTRODUCTION

Whenever the history of Indo-Polish relations in the first half of the twentieth century is discussed, names of interesting personalities like Wanda Dynowska[1] and Moritz Friedman[2] are mentioned or the story of Polish war refugees accommodated in Kolhapur and Jamnagar colonies[3] is narrated.

Interesting as these stories and persons are, they should be seen in their real perspective and dimensions as far as the relations between the states of India and Poland are concerned.

The purpose of this paper is to bring forward new documents constituting historical evidence of a practically forgotten event, which may be however considered as a valid point of reference in drawing conclusions on the history of Indo-Polish relations in terms of realpolitik.

This event is the visit of Subhas Chandra Bose to Poland in July 1933.

Subhas Chandra Bose is hardly known in Poland beyond a narrow circle of academics interested in the Indian history of the twentieth century. I think it is also quite common in many other countries where the permanently repeated narration of M. K. Gandhi and Jawaharlal Nehru's legends of freedom fighting have created a virtual monopoly of discourse and personalities whenever India's independence is discussed.

In recent years the thoughts and visions presented by Subhas Chandra Bose are more often present in public space. I am convinced this process will continue in future.

It is in this context that I have considered it interesting to research the reasons of Subhas Chandra Bose's visit to Poland. I am not satisfied with statements that Bose admired Poland for its struggle for independence, etc. His historical knowledge was vast, so certainly it was true, but such admiration or interest in the mind of a politician and visionary like Bose could be just a raw material for creating a tangible product of realpolitik.

The beginning of 1933 found Subhas Chandra Bose a prisoner of the Raj and a very ill prisoner he was.

SUBHAS CHANDRA BOSE'S
TRIP TO EUROPE IN 1933

When on August 22, 1930 Subhas Chandra Bose was elected the Mayor of Calcutta no one could possibly predict that in less than eighteen months not only would his service in that capacity be terminated but he would be imprisoned and, due to the deterioration of his health, the manner of his further struggle for free India would become an unknown factor.

Subhas Chandra Bose was arrested after the series of events in Dhaka and Chittagong and his active involvement in the protests against the Raj.[4]

He served as the Mayor during a period of internal troubles in the Congress Party in Bengal which included his differences with J. M. Sengupta.[5] This together with his relations with Mahatma Gandhi was building a momentum and for the first time presenting Bose with a dilemma (yet not the last as the future would prove) in which going abroad seemed to be a valid, if not the only reasonable option.

On a number of occasions Subhas Chandra Bose used to emphasize that the question of India's future was not a bilateral matter between India and Great Britain.

In his letter from Vienna written on July 7, 1933, just before departing for Prague, Bose wrote:

In international economics and international politics, the Indian question is allowed to be treated as a domestic question between England and India in which the world at large has no right to interfere. But India should not take this position lying down. India is entitled to bring her case before the bar of the world opinion. In this connection I desire to urge upon my countrymen the dire necessity of appointing accredited representatives of India in foreign countries. Even if representatives cannot be sent out from India owing to lack of funds there are Indians abroad who would be prepared to work even for love ... and without international propaganda India cannot possibly establish itself in the eyes of the world.[6]

It may be noted that in any source to which I have had an access, Bose did not refer to the activities of Indians in the continental Europe in the first two decades of the twentieth century, notably the Berlin Committee founded in 1914 and renamed in 1915 as the India Independence Committee which conducted its activity until 1918, or Madame B. R. Cama[7] and her well-known appearance at the Socialist International Meeting in Stuttgart[8] in 1907.

These events and efforts may be considered as presenting the Indian case before the world much earlier than Bose's foregoing remarks.

In fact what Subhas Chandra Bose proposes in his above quoted letter from Vienna is establishing the institution of some kind of "Honorary Consuls" of India. This in my opinion is the meaning of "accredited representatives"—Indians abroad who would "work for love."

Bose was arrested at the beginning of January 1932 and then transferred several times to different prisons. His health deteriorated seriously and in December 1932 the Medical Board recommended that he should go to the Calcutta Medical College and later to Switzerland for treatment.

Still a prisoner, Subhas Chandra Bose boarded or, rather, was brought on stretchers to the SS Ganges which left Bombay on February 23, 1933.

He landed in Venice on March 6, 1933 and on March 8, 1933 he was already in Vienna.

Preparations for visiting a number of European states was one of the activities Bose undertook while in Vienna. His passport—he was a British subject thus holding a passport issued by the British authorities—was not valid for the United Kingdom, which in itself is an extraordinary matter worth a study on passport procedures.

The British consular service in Vienna endorsed Bose's passport for a number of countries of Europe. Poland was not among the states which, by the decision taken by the British mission in Vienna, Bose was allowed to visit. However Czechoslovakia was.

SUBHAS CHANDRA BOSE
IN THE EMBASSY OF POLAND IN VIENNA

During his visit to Prague Bose approached the British mission for endorsing his passport for Poland, Belgium, Holland and Egypt. All except Egypt were granted.

It seems that the idea of visiting Poland may have materialised in Bose's mind only after his visit to the Embassy of Poland in Vienna at the end of June 1933. This suggestion is based upon the statement in the letter from the Embassy of June 28, 1933 as discussed below. At that time Bose had already twice requested the British mission in Vienna for stamping permission in his passport to visit a number of countries.

Both approaches (March 25 and April 24, 1933) were successful. Yet Poland was on neither list of Bose's requests. It may be assumed that initially he had no definite plans for visiting Poland. He only applied in Prague to the British Consul for passport endorsement and to the Polish Consul for the visa. Both attempts were successful.[9]

On June 28, 1933 the Charge d'Affaires in the Embassy of Poland in Vienna Mr. M. Moscicki dispatched a letter to the State Export Institute in Warsaw, with copies to two departments: the Ministry of Foreign Affairs of Poland and the Ministry of Industry. (Attachment no. 1)

As the letter did not specify the date of Bose's visit to the Embassy we have to be content with presuming that it took place at the end of June 1933.

The report on Bose's visit to the Embassy in Vienna is in my opinion a solid material for evaluating a scope and directions of his interest in Poland.

As we read in the first lines of the letter from the Embassy (attached with its translation into English) Subhas Chandra Bose expressed vivid interest in Poland and requested all possible information about Polish products, which could find demand in East India, especially in Calcutta, where Mr. Bose was a city mayor for a long time.[10] We may skip disputing whether Bose was the Mayor of Calcutta for a long time, but we should note that Bose came to the meeting in the Embassy with a ready list of products from Poland, which were to find demand on the Indian market. These products listed by Bose were: cotton products, artificial silk, paper, cement, sugar, lubricating oils, paraffin, agricultural machines, pipes for gas and water lines, railway cars and locomotives, rails, enamelware, alcohol spirits and hops.

It may be the subject of further research to find upon whose advice Bose compiled the list. Such indications could only be prepared by individuals or institutions like Chambers of Commerce directly involved in the commercial life of Calcutta and India. During his service as the Mayor (as well as earlier as CEO of the Calcutta administration of Chittaranjan Das[11]) Bose had easy access to the commerce and industry community of Calcutta, Bengal and the whole of India.

It may also be presumed that the list of products for trade with India was considered also for other countries.

So the first contact Bose made with Poland was not much emotional in its nature nor did it refer to Poland's independence struggle, a love of country, oriental studies and the like.

On the contrary Bose came to the Embassy (with his secretary, as he is referred to, Mr. I. S. Mathur) with a business proposal of establishing commercial ties concerning precisely defined products.

Yet, in my opinion, this specific proposal for commercial relations shows Subhas Chandra Bose to be a visionary much better than any rhetoric on freedom fighting and revolutionary ideas could do.

Bose was aware that the second half of the nineteenth century and the first three decades of the twentieth century were a period of an intensive development of orientalist interest in India as well as strengthening of the perception of India as the land of esoteric mysteries, spiritual traditions which the Europeans looked upon either with excitement and sectarian admiration or with contempt. However in many cases it was just a shrug of shoulders over some barbaric, heathen rituals.

Subhas Chandra Bose talked to Polish diplomats in Vienna in 1933 about business between Polish and Indian partners.

Bose also expressed his desire to see into the possibilities of selling Indian products in Poland.

He came as a representative of India's cause and Indian economic potential rather than as representing a state and an existing political administration entity.

It may be stated that the diplomats at the Embassy of Poland in Vienna were impressed by Bose and his proposals.

Not only did they advise Bose to visit Poland (see the letter) but the Embassy immediately issued recommendation letters to the Director of the State Export Institute in Warsaw, to the Chamber of Commerce and Industry in Warsaw and to the Central Union of Polish Industry, Commerce, Mining and Finances.

As Bose's trip to Prague took place on June 29, 1933 (by plane from Vienna) there was no time for additional passport endorsement and arranging of Polish visa.

Embassies are not generally known for enthusiastic distribution of their support letters.

The interest shown by the officials of the Polish Embassy in Vienna in Bose's proposals and their support for him may be viewed as the Embassy's initiative undertaken with a full knowledge that he was not only a former official in the colonial structure of British administration but also—as we read in the very first sentence of the letter in question—"Chairman of Congress in Bengalia." The word "Bengalia" is used in the letter therefore I leave it without any corrections.

SUBHAS CHANDRA BOSE IN WARSAW

Subhas Chandra Bose arrived in Warsaw on July 7, 1933 and stayed in the Hotel Bruhl on Freta Street no. 12.[12]

From the hotel Bose wrote to Mme Naomi C. Vetter that he planned to stay in Warsaw for 8 days and would be leaving for Berlin by train on July 17, 1933.[13]

In his later references to the visit to Poland Bose had nothing but kind and warm words about the country and people he met.

In his letter to Santosh Kumar Basu dated March 14, 1934 Bose recollected his visit to Warsaw and wrote that he was received at the City Hall by the Deputy Mayor of Warsaw with whom he had a cordial talk; a photo taken during the meeting was printed in a Polish newspaper. Bose was shown not only around the City Hall offices but also visited the gas works, the bakery that produced bread for one-third of the city and the Warsaw Physical Culture Institute which made a good impression on him.[14]

Another line of Bose's activities during his visit to Warsaw, the only line known to some extent in Poland, is his interaction with scholars of the University of Warsaw.

The name of Stanisław Franciszek Michalski (also known as Stanisław Franciszek Michalski-Iwienski)[15] is practically always mentioned whenever Bose's visit to Poland is discussed.

Michalski was a well-known Polish researcher in the Sanskrit language, an author of many books and translations of original Sanskrit texts into the Polish language. Bose praised Prof. Michalski as well as the Polish people in general for being "wide awake" and having an attitude "of sympathy for India's struggle for national emancipation."

The quotation comes from the article titled "A friend of India in Poland" which Bose published in April 1936 in *The Modern Review*, a Calcutta paper. This friend was Professor Michalski himself.[16]

In the same article Bose concluded: "The ground has already been prepared for a Polish-Indian Society in Poland with a corresponding branch in India. All that is wanted now is that someone should take the lead."[17]

Bose mentioned also Prof. Stasiak of the Lvov Academic Centre. Bose remembered the warm hospitality of Prof. Michalski who presented him "a bundle of his own publications."

While in Poland Subhas Chandra Bose proposed to establish the Indo-Polish Society. He made the same proposal during his visit to Prague (Indo-Czechoslovakian Society) and in 1934 the Society was inaugurated in Prague. Industrial groups like Skoda and Bata were the active part of this project.

This initiative in Poland did not work out.

It is true that in 1936 the Bharata Mitra Parishad was founded in Warsaw. The organisation was mentioned in the Indian press as "the Indian Museum in Poland"[18] (attachment no. 2); its goal was first and foremost to promote culture and mutual knowledge.

This was far from what Bose had in mind when he talked to Polish diplomats in Vienna in 1933.

FOLLOW-UP FROM EMBASSY OF POLAND IN VIENNA AND CONSULATE OF POLAND IN BOMBAY ON BOSE'S PROPOSALS

The visit of Subhas Chandra Bose to Poland was followed by an exchange of correspondence between the Polish missions in Vienna and Bombay and the Polish central institutions like the Ministry of Foreign Affairs, Polish Institute of Export and Eastern Institute of Poland.

The correspondence allows us to give a realistic evaluation of Indo-Polish relations in the 1930s.

I shall also bring forward for comparison a classified report on India elaborated in August 1944 by a high-ranking Polish diplomat responsible for advising and creating the policy of the Polish Government in Exile towards India.

The documents quoted in this paper will present the position of the state institutions of Poland in the 1930s concerning India's emancipation efforts.

The Embassy of Poland in Vienna sent a letter addressed to the Ministry of Foreign Affairs (Department No. III) in Warsaw. This letter ref. no.352/tj/A/1 is dated August 11, 1934 and signed by Mr. S. Lalicki, the Commercial Counselor.[19] (Attachment no. 3)

Copies of this letter were sent to the Polish Institute of Export, to the Department No. II of the Ministry of Foreign Affairs and to the Embassy in London. India as a British colony was in the jurisdiction of the Polish Embassy in London.

So, in 1933 the newly established Consulate of Poland in Bombay was reporting to the Embassy in London and not to the Ministry in Poland.

The letter contained references to the conferences conducted by Mr. Bose in the Embassy in Vienna and to his visit to Warsaw undertaken upon their initiative[20] as well as a detailed description of the Indian Central

European Society located in Vienna. Mr. Lalicki informed that Mr. Bose was still in contact with the Embassy and wrote:

> ... From the words of Mr. Bose and his companions it should be assumed that he and his organisation are vividly interested in establishing relations between Poland and India. Mr. Faltis (MM: Otto Faltis, Chairman of the Oesterreichische Escompteverband in Vienna) has already prepared a draft of two chapters of the branch organisation namely the Indian Central European Society for Poland. This Society according to the author, would only be very generally associated with the Vienna organisation, i.e., persons from the Vienna organisation would assist in creation of its Polish chapter. The development of economic relations between Poland and India would be conducted by direct contacts between the two countries.

> Our Embassy has suggested that the Eastern Institute together with the Union of Chambers of Commerce in Warsaw could take action in creating the above-mentioned organisation.

> Mr. Bose and his organisation are now awaiting specific proposals from the Polish side ....[21]

In the letter with ref. no. L/352/tj/A/2 dated October 20, 1934[22] the Embassy of Poland requests the Ministry of Foreign Affairs of Poland if "the competent Polish partners (Eastern Institute and possibly the Union of Chambers of Commerce in Warsaw) have already made a decision to establish a similar Indo-Polish organisation." (Attachment no. 4).

Naturally the Consulate of Poland in Bombay was informed about Bose's initiative towards Poland and the Consul of Poland, Mr. Eugeniusz Banasiński[23] enquired on that matter in his correspondence.

Mr. Banasiński sent to the Ministry of Foreign Affairs letters expressing his interest and opinions about the initiatives of Subhas Chandra Bose regarding his visit to Poland.

I would like to bring forward two pieces of correspondence between the Consul in Bombay and the Ministry of Foreign Affairs in Warsaw. In his

IFPS OCCASIONAL PAPER SERIES, NO. 5

letter with ref. no. 351-b/1/pf dated May 16, 1934[24] (Attachment no. 5), Mr. Banasiński wrote:

> The Reuters agency informs on May 3 (MM—1934) that there was a meeting in Vienna in the Vienna Chamber of Commerce where the Indo-Central European Association for commercial and cultural relations between India and Austria was established. Former minister Pest was presiding and Mr. Bose was also present. Mr. Bose is about to leave for Prague to establish a similar organisation there. With reference to the above please kindly advise me on Mr. Bose's efforts to establish further contacts with us and at what stage is his initiative which was presented last year in the Eastern Institute regarding the establishment of the Indo-Polish association.
>
> The already established Austro-Indian association is said to have already started in its premises a permanent exhibition of Indian products and intends to organise the Indian pavilion at the autumn Vienna Fair with special emphasis on Indian agriculture and mineral raw materials.

The Polish Consul informed his principals in Warsaw and London about the tangible shapes the initiatives of Subhas Chandra Bose were taking in Vienna and Prague and requested a follow-up of such initiatives with reference to Poland.

Mr. Banasiński continued his requests and clear support for Bose's ideas in his letter with ref. no. 351-b/4 dated November 22, 1934[25] (Attachment no. 6) addressed to the Polish Institute of Export with copies to his superiors in Warsaw and London.

We can quote from pages 3 and 4 of the letter as below:

> We should bear in mind that the whole of India, no matter of what political direction, realises how much their economic life is suppressed by the English policy of preferences and quasi protection. They will willingly see (there is also a political element in this) commercial proposals from other countries aimed at weakening the economic strength of England in India.

IFPS OCCASIONAL PAPER SERIES, NO. 5

It is this element that in my opinion plays an essential role in the concepts of Mr. Bose as far as the economic matters are concerned.

Therefore I think that by creating a Polish-Indian economic and cultural association we can only win but never lose, especially when the action of Mr. Bose will find lively response in the self-government economic institutions of India and when they will start cooperating in that activity. This cooperation, as I see it, would take shape of introducing economy of this or other country into the territory of India and to influence the mind of an Indian merchant and industrialist in order to seek relations without political conflicts. ... Bearing this in mind I do not suppose that the possible Polish-Indian association could stand in contradiction and conflict with works of currently operating commercial network in India. On the contrary I think that it will be very helpful and especially if the proposals of Mr. Bose will find support in the self-governing commercial entities of India. If during the future activities of the association, new forces would emerge aiming at some practical commercial tasks, then I am convinced that there is sufficient volume of work to be done.

I even think that we should actively support and act towards such aims, as both the work of the Consulate and the existing business infrastructure, in spite of much efforts and work, is not capable to cover the region equivalent in size to Europe.[26]

We have gone through the correspondence between the Embassy of Poland in Vienna and the Consulate in Bombay, the two foreign missions of Poland which were actively involved in the subject of Bose's visit to Poland.

Apart from issuing the visa for Mr. Bose to enter Poland, the Embassy in Prague responded to the request of the Ministry of Foreign Affairs to comment on the visit of Bose to Czechoslovakia in 1934.

This was his second visit and he came practically only for a day to inaugurate the Indo-Czechoslovakian Association. In his letter to the Ministry of Foreign Affairs, ref. no. 352/C/2 of July 27, 1934, the Counsellor of the Embassy Mr. Zygmunt Hladki informed:

IFPS OCCASIONAL PAPER SERIES, NO. 5

... apart from establishing personal contacts with groups interested in India, his [S. C. Bose—MM] visit in Prague did not leave any results. He did not establish any contacts apart from meeting with members of economic communities. As he is also a radical politician close to Ghandi [spelling as in the letter of the Embassy] he was treated with proper caution.[27]

The Embassy of Poland was clearly misinformed about Bose's established relations and meetings and since it is not my intention do discuss Bose's visits to Czechoslovakia I will leave the subject at this point.

We may say that both the Embassy in Vienna and the Consulate in Bombay were convinced supporters of promoting Bose's idea of developing relations with Poland.

The first and foremost field of that cooperation as seen by Bose as well as the Polish missions in Vienna and Bombay were economic and business relations.

CENTRAL INSTITUTIONS IN WARSAW
AND BOSE'S PROPOSALS

Three central Polish institutions were involved in considering Subhas Chandra Bose's proposals as communicated in the dispatches of the Embassy of Poland in Vienna. These institutions received the proposals in writing from the Polish missions and therefore were expected to respond officially. They did it, however not without a written follow-up from the original conveyor of information.

The Eastern Institute was seen by the Embassy in Vienna and the Consulate in Bombay as the body which would mobilise the Chambers of Commerce and establish the Indo-Polish Association.

Its response was crucial to further evaluations.

In response to enquiries from the Ministry of Foreign Affairs and missions in Vienna and Bombay the Director of the Eastern Institute Prof. Dr. Olgierd Górka sent the letter with ref. no. 113-34r of August 6, 1934 (Attachment no. 7) to the Ministry of Foreign Affairs-Eastern Department.

Director Górka informed:

> ... the matter of the Polish-Indian Society has been in a dead point since the time of the visit of the ex-Mayor of Calcutta, Subhas Chandra Bose, the reason being that he did not fulfil his promise of returning to Warsaw. In effect the initiative presented was waiting for the promised return in few weeks or two months. Additionally other supporting voices in the matter, for example from Mr. St. Hulanicki, did not seem to sound serious enough. The Eastern Institute did not so far undertake any action to organise such a society. This would require first of all some promotion, communication with professor Stasiak in Lvov, Professor Willman-Grabowska in Krakow, etc. Of course we can organise it in two or three weeks if only the Ministry of Foreign Affairs will approve this initiative which at the moment is not pursued.[28]

That letter was attached to the dispatch from the Ministry of Foreign Affairs Political Department and sent to the Consulate of Poland in Bombay and two Departments of the Ministry.

The letter with ref. no. P.III.352/1-A/4 dated August 10, 1934[29] was signed by Mr. Jan Wszelaki, the Deputy Director of the Political Department. (Attachment no. 8)

After references to previous communications the Ministry of Foreign Affairs wrote:

> ... At the same time the Ministry would like to inform the subject of organising the Polish-Indian Society will be considered in case the Indian side and Mr. Bose will approach us again.

The State Export Institute which was also to be instrumental in the formation of relations with India as per Bose's and the Embassy in Vienna proposal presented its opinion in two letters attached to this paper.

Mr. M. Turski, the Director of the Polish Institute of Export, in his letter ref. no. E/27034/3.D of October 31, 1934 (Attachment 9) sent to the Ministry of Foreign Affairs referred directly to Bose's proposals as presented in the letters of the Embassy in Vienna:

> With reference to reports of the Polish Embassy in Vienna ... and earlier correspondence about the Indian institutions in Austria and their interest in Polish-Indian economic relations the Polish Institute of Export advises to exercise great caution while dealing with these matters ....[30]

At the end the Institute suggested the Consulate in Bombay should check the matter in details.

As we know from the above presented earlier correspondence, the Consulate presented its evaluation in the letter of May 16, 1934 and confirmed it in the letter of November 22, 1934.

Even after the evaluation of the Consulate in Bombay of November 22, 1934, the Polish Institute of Export in another letter of Director M. Turski

IFPS OCCASIONAL PAPER SERIES, NO. 5

ref. no. E/32023/3.D. of December 18, 1934[31] (Attachment no. 10) addressed to the Ministry of Foreign Affairs stated:

> ... Polish Institute of Export is of the opinion that the proposed by Mr. Bose, Polish-Indian organisation may indeed have positive influence on our economic relations with India and the Institute will gladly cooperate with such organisation. However, we think that such organisation should rather have general goals, i.e., cultural, political, etc., and so should be established by a similar Polish institution. Our Institute is of the opinion that the Eastern Institute should organise the said society ...[32]

As we know from the above-mentioned earlier correspondence the Eastern Institute did not take any action because S. C. Bose did not come back again to Poland (sic!). However the Institute would be willing to do it, if the Ministry of Foreign Affairs considered it wise.

But the Ministry of Foreign Affairs stated they could consider the matter only if Mr. Bose approached them again.

This in a colloquial language is the story of communications among the Polish central institutions on the proposals of S. C. Bose. They were clearly not interested.

The above quotations and remarks point to the differences of attitudes and evaluations between the Polish foreign missions and the central institutions of Poland. This will be elaborated in the concluding remarks.

ESTABLISHING THE CONSULATE OF
POLAND IN BOMBAY—1933

Poland's historical interests in Asia may be considered in terms of its relations with Persia, Turkey and maybe episodically with Japan.

Anything beyond that will be transplanting stories of individuals and events that came out as a third party's actions into the state to the state or people-to-people relations, which is not justified, no matter how pleasant these stories may be. This has been already stated at the beginning of this paper.

It may be well understood that for Poland, which emerged as an independent state in 1918 after 123 years of lost statehood, relations with South Asia were not a priority.

Nevertheless the interest of Poland in South Asia region was developing and in 1933 the first ever Polish Consulate in the region was established.

It was the Consulate in Bombay and Mr. Eugeniusz Banasiński was nominated as a Consul of Poland; later he was promoted to the rank of Consul General. It may be interesting to note that the next diplomat to hold the rank of Consul General as the head of the Bombay mission was the author of this article at the beginning of the twenty-first century.

Mr. Banasiński was recalled from his post in the Embassy of Poland in Tokyo to lead the new Consulate.

The purpose of establishing the post in Bombay was to encourage, develop and organise economic and business relations between Polish and Indian companies.

There is a significant volume of documents available concerning the business promotion activities of Mr. Banasiński and the Consulate. Even though he did not have any specific prior knowledge or experience of India, his reports and letters showed not only a good sense of judgement but also elements of visualising India as a significant player in the post-Second World War times.

If the Polish authorities undertook such efforts and borne costs to make a foundation for economic and business relations with India (the Consulate in Bombay) then the opinions of the Polish central institutions of Bose's proposals of 1933 may come as a surprise.

INDIA AS A PART OF THE BRITISH DISCOURSE OF THE POLISH FOREIGN POLICY IN THE 1930S

When we read the correspondence of the Polish central institutions, we find that Subhas Chandra Bose is always referred to as the ex-Mayor or the ex-Deputy Mayor of Calcutta. He held the posts in the colonial administration structure made by the British, thus he was a part of the British order in India.

In Warsaw he was also received by the Deputy Mayor of Warsaw which corresponded to one of the posts Bose had and the way he was referred to in Poland.

In other words, should anyone from the British side enquire why Poland dealt with a person openly opposing the British Raj, the answer was clear and ready. Subhas Chandra Bose was received in Poland only in his capacity as the ex-Mayor or the Deputy Mayor of Calcutta. He held these posts within the Raj, the British administration machinery. So obviously this was sufficient to see him as a component of the British system.

Other aspects of Bose's activities and concepts were beyond the interest of any Polish central institutions.

This was not the case with his visits to Czechoslovakia in 1933, 1934 and 1938 where apart from the City Mayor of Prague Bose was received inter alia by the Minister of Foreign Affairs.

His position in the Congress Party and references to his activity as an independence fighter were mentioned in the letter from the Embassy in Vienna and in the correspondence from the Consulate in Bombay.

The proposals of Subhas Chandra Bose regarding developing business contacts were in line with the directions and guidelines given to the Consulate of Poland in Bombay. The Consul himself considered the proposals a good idea, as we have read in the communications quoted above.

Yet the initiative was given a cold shoulder, to use the phrase, and the highest Polish institutions responsible for foreign affairs and business promotion were not interested in them.

The answer to the question as to why that was so must be based upon a statement that in Poland's foreign policy of the 1930s India was a part of the British discourse and not a concept based on dealings or visualising future dealings with an independent entity—i.e., the independent Indian state.

Thus all the arrangements made with Great Britain including establishing a Consulate of Poland fitted perfectly the development of relations with Great Britain.

It may be well understood that the Eurocentric foreign policy of Poland in the interwar period, i.e., also in the 1930s, was essential. Also relations with Germany and Soviet Russia had to be somehow balanced with what appeared to Warsaw as a friendly alliance with England and France.

What may be noted is the lack of provisions in the foreign policy of Poland for constructing alternative visions of future for the next 2-3 decades.

Extrapolation, i.e., continuity of a known existing political set-up and political qualities, was the only stream followed by the foreign policy institutions of Poland.

Subhas Chandra Bose, when talking to Polish diplomats in Vienna, was in a way a visitor from the future. He was not a component of the British discourse. On the contrary he represented "the Indian cause," a political and economic quality of the future. That quality did not fit the receptive capabilities of Polish political thought in the 1930s.

One may also take into account the possibility of Bose's proposals just encountering wrong persons in the central Polish institutions at that particular time and that it was a kind of bad luck.

In order to check the validity of the above indications on Polish foreign policy, I decided to bring forward one more document. This document is from 1944, i.e., a decade after Bose's proposals were made.

IFPS OCCASIONAL PAPER SERIES, NO. 5

A POLISH DIPLOMAT WRITES
ABOUT INDIA IN 1944

In 1944 the Polish mission in Chungking in the Chiang Kai-shek held territories of China, had the diplomatic jurisdiction over British India. The Embassy was responsible to the Polish Government in Exile in London.

The letter quoted by me (Attachment no. 11) was classified by the author and marked as "secret."[33]

It is dated August 22, 1944 with ref. no. Nr.Ch 3.13.44, signed by Ambassador Alfred Poninski[34] and addressed to "The Minister of Foreign Affairs—London."

Mr. Tadeusz Romer was the Minister of Foreign Affairs in the Government in Exile at that time.

In order to evaluate the line of thinking, as presented in Mr. Poninski's letter, it should be stated that by August 1944 a significant portion of Polish territory was already under the control of the Soviet Union with the pro-Soviet Polish administration coming into existence on July 22, 1944. The Warsaw Uprising—one of the tragic events of Polish history—was struggling against Germans, with no hope for help from any of the Allies.

However, the most important element of the political scenario against which the guidelines and thoughts of Ambassador Poninski must be read is that almost a year passed since the Tehran Conference—November 28, 1943-December 1, 1943[35]—where the "Big Three" (W. Churchill, F. D. Roosevelt and J. V. Stalin) had agreed with regard to Poland that after the War it would be ruled by a Soviet friendly government and its Eastern border would be the Curzon line[36] (which the Soviet Union demanded). It was also agreed that these matters would be revealed neither to the public nor to the Polish Government in Exile in London. The fate of Poland was sealed a few months later in Yalta.

With the above in mind we can quote from the above-mentioned letter: I take the liberty to submit to you Mr. Minister, in this communication a number of my own observations on the essential changes taking place in India. My opinions are derived practically exclusively from discussions with people taking direct part in shaping the present picture of India as well as on my own subjective impressions, after my few months of visiting such distant places like Calcutta, Madras, Bombay, Delhi and also the last year visit to Karachi.

British or other authors, whose equally subjective opinions are usually considered to be objective information material, in most cases got acquainted with one or two of the above centres as tourists and were lacking local contacts which I managed to find along the whole route.

That is why I feel encouraged to put forward opinions significantly differing from common publications in the British and other Allies press.

While preparing this report my main idea was to give to the Ministry comments on the phenomena in the Indian politics and Indo-British relations, which are not understood by the common continental mind, even more that the available literature on the subject is either questionable or extremely partisan due to the *a priori* attitude of the authors.

It is a fact that this very significant problem of the future is being presented to the United Nations in a false manner of concepts and ideas not taking into account in a sufficient way the Indian reality which only few Britons managed to comprehend.

I suppose that as an ally of Great Britain we should avoid repeating in the subject of the future of the British Empire, light and trivial approaches and that it is necessary that our official sources should have elements enabling the understanding of a very complex policy

IFPS OCCASIONAL PAPER SERIES, NO. 5

of our British ally in this respect, which as a conclusion should be of assistance in the current diplomatic cooperation between Poland and Britain.

If we can show understanding of the Indian problems better than other allies, we shall gain greatly as a Government and in the area of diplomacy in the evaluations of the responsible British authorities. We cannot disregard possible practical benefits which this will give us in the period of setting a new world order after defeating the totalitarian forces of the Axis.

Our own light-heartedness, ill-located sentimentalism, alien suggestions, permanently coming from anti-British sources and the partisan British and Indian literature on Indian matters, have continuous influence on the shaping of Polish public opinion and cause statements which cannot be compatible with our or British basic interest.

The evil which comes out of this is not contradicted by anyone. Our mission in India was so far a retarded administrative unit, organically unable to initiate any action to draw the attention of our responsible centres to tremendous consequences of our Government not reacting to seemingly small Polish mistakes, offences and nuances, in India as well as on the platform of theoretical statements.

Letting the Poles come to India was an act of exceptional trust in us from the central British authorities and what is more important from the British authorities in India, with their influence on the great Imperial politics which is permanent and direct in contrast to the changing attitudes of London offices....

(By ref 3-MM—it was agreed by the British authorities, Polish Government in exile and the involvement of two Maharajas that about 6,000 people, children, women and older men who left the Soviet Union with the Polish army of General W. Anders in 1942, will be placed in two specially prepared camp-colonies in Kolhapur and Jamnagar. This was an entirely humanitarian action. We will never know what Mr. Poninski had in mind saying that taking these children and women into India was the "act of exceptional trust" to Poles.)

> ... I take the liberty of posing the question if we realise this sufficiently and whether our Government offices deciding upon current refugee, administrative and personal matters, etc., take this into consideration at all.

> India is not some kind of Cyprus or Kenya (MM—please note the contempt for smaller states), where words of criticism or light remarks of guests from abroad on local relations, administration, etc., are passed without comments, as these things are really of no care to the English.

> If already today the administration of India exerts great influence upon the imperial politics as a whole then tomorrow after the establishment of a real self-rule or few ambitious self-ruling governments always tied with Great Britain with knots of defence, commerce and currency, that role will be much bigger and we will be sorry that we could not make use of the possibilities the War gave us to strengthen the positive attitudes and opinions on Poland necessary for developing economic cooperation, etc.

The British oriented subaltern thinking with no regard for the emerging world order and new qualities coming with it are the characteristics of the statements in the above letter as well as of the policy built upon the priority of pleasing the alleged ally as a leading guideline in the foreign policy.

The quoted letter may be used in a debate on Polish foreign policy in the pre-war and war period, yet the reason of bringing it forward in this paper is only to state that the British discourse in a wide sector of the foreign policy of Poland was not a characteristic referring only to the case of Bose's proposals in 1933 but it was its permanent characteristic even in the circumstances when a re-evaluation of that subalternity was a matter of an urgent necessity, as was the case in 1944.

IFPS OCCASIONAL PAPER SERIES, NO. 5

CONCLUSION

The newly found documents enable us to put a statement that Bose's visit to Poland in 1933 was considered by him first of all as an opportunity to establish direct contacts of promoting economic and business relations between Polish and Indian partners. Since the proposal was coming from sources out of the British control, it was not taken for continuation by the Polish central institutions as shown in the letters presented. This lack of continuation took place in spite of Polish efforts to promote business with India conducted via channels entirely agreed with the British side (i.e., establishing the Consulate in Bombay in 1933).

The visit of Subhas Chandra Bose to Poland in 1933 may be seen as the first attempt to put the relations between India and Poland on a modern partnership track beyond academic and sentimental ties.

Notes
1. Wanda Dynowska (Umadevi) (June 30, 1888-March 20, 1971) Polish theosophist, writer, translator, publisher, social activist, promoter of intercultural exchanges between India and Poland, founded the Indian-Polish Library in Bombay.
2. Moritz Friedman or in Polish, Maurycy Frydman, also known as Swami Bharatananda (born in 1901 in Warsaw, died, March 9, 1977 in India), was an engineer and humanist who spent the later part of his life in India. He lived at the ashram of Gandhi and took part in India's independence efforts, i.e., he helped to draft a new constitution for the State of Audh. He was a student of Maharaj Nissergadatta and translated his lectures into English.
3. In the first half of 1942 the soldiers of the Polish army of General W. Anders and civilians left the Soviet Union (about 40 thousand soldiers and 10 thousand civilians). The Polish Government in Exile in agreement with the British authorities and assistance of two princely states (Maharajas of Kolhapur and Jamnagar) organised two camp colonies for them. These camps were opened in Valivade in the Kolhapur state and Balachadi in the state of Jamnagar.

4. http://en.wikipedia.org/wiki/Chittagong_armoury_raid.
5. Jatindra Mohan Sengupta, 1885-1933, Congress Party activist and leader in Bengal. Opponent of S. C. Bose.
6. Mihir Bose, *The Lost Hero—A Biography of Subhas Bose*, (Noida, India: Wide Canvas, 2014), p. 135.
7. Bhikaiji Rusto Cama (September 24, 1861-August 13, 1936) a prominent figure in the Indian independence movement.
8. International Socialist Congress, Stuttgart, 1907, 7th Congress of the Second International. It was held in Stuttgart, Germany from August 18 to 24, 1907 and attended by almost 900 delegates from around the globe. The work of the congress dealt largely with matters of militarism, colonialism, and women's suffrage and marked an attempt to centrally coordinate the policies of the various socialist parties of the world on these issues. It was there that Madame B. R. Cama unfurled the flag of independent India.
9. Sugata Bose, *His Majesty's Opponent—Subhas Chandra Bose and India's Struggle against Empire*, Gurgaon, Haryana, India: Penguin Books, 2013), p. 90.
10. Letter no.57/A/a/2 dated June 28, 1933 Embassy of Poland in Vienna as in attachment no 1.
11. Chittaranjan Das (popularly known as Deshbandhu, "Friend of the country") (born November 5, 1870-died June 16, 1925) was an Indian politician and founder-leader of the Swaraj (Independence) Party in Bengal under British rule. When the Calcutta Municipal Corporation was formed, he became its first Mayor.
12. Hotel Bruhl. This hotel does not exist anymore. It was destroyed during the Warsaw Uprising in 1944.
13. *Netaji Collected Works*, Volume 8: *India's Ambassador Abroad: Letters, articles, speeches and statements, 1933-1937*, Calcutta: 1994, p. 45.
14. *His Majesty's Opponent...*, pp. 90-91, cited in *Netaji Collected Works*, vol. 8, p. 57.
15. Stanisław Franciszek Michalski, born on January 29, 1881 in Tarnogrod, died on August 8, 1961 in Lodz, Polish indologist, encyclopedist. Translated texts from Sanskrit and Pali, i.e. fragments of *Rigweda,* the *Upanishads* and *Bhagavad Gita*, as well as Buddhist texts, i.e. *Dhammapada*.
16. *Modern Review* was the name of a monthly magazine published in Calcutta since 1907. Founded by Ramananda Chatterjee, the *Modern Review* soon emerged as an important forum for the Indian Nationalist Intelligentsia, Wikipedia, *Modern Review*, December 27, 2014.
17. Ibid.
18. *The Bombay Sentinel*, June 1936, as in attachment 2.
19. Embassy of Poland in Vienna, letter no. 352/tj/A/1 dated August 11, 1934 (Attachment no. 3).
20. Ibid.
21. Ibid.
22. Letter L/352/tj/A/2 dated October 20, 1934 as in attachment no. 4.
23. Eugeniusz Banasiński, born December 9, 1886 in Poland, died on January 1, 1964 in

Bombay. Polish diplomat. First Polish Consul General in Bombay.

24. Letter no. 351-b/1/pf, dated May 16, 1934 as in Attachment no. 5.
25. Letter no. 351-b/4 dated November 22, 1934 as in Attachment no. 6.
26. Ibid.
27. Letter number 352/C/2 dated July 27, 1934.
28. Letter no. 1113-34 dated August 6, 1934.
29. Letter no. P.III.352/1-A/4 dated August 10, 1934 as in attachment 8.
30. Letter no. E/27034/3.D dated October 31, 1934 as in Attachment no. 9.
31. Letter no. E/32023/3.D. dated December 18, 1934 as in attachment 10.
32. Ibid.
33. Letter no. Nr.Ch 3.13.44 dated August 22, 1944 as in Attachment no. 11.
34. Alfred Emeryk Poniński, born on June 18, 1896 in Poland, died on March 25, 1968 in Sydney, Polish diplomat and journalist dealing almost entirely with European affairs. In December 1942 he was designated as the first Ambassador of Poland in the Republic of China with Chiang Kai-shek in Chungqing. This was his first contact with Asia. He was the ambassador till July 1945 when the Government of Poland in Exile ceased to be recognised by the Allies and most of the UNO states. After the Second World War he immigrated to Australia.
35. http://en.wikipedia.org/wiki/Tehran_Conference.
36. The Curzon Line was put forward by the Supreme War Council after World War I as the demarcation line between the Second Polish Republic and Bolshevik Russia, and was supposed to serve as the basis for a future border. The Soviet Union during the WWII was in favour of establishing the Curzon Line as the Eastern border of Poland. This indeed took place.

Literature

1. Mihir Bose, *The Lost Hero—Biography of Subhas Bose*, (Noida, India: Wide Canvas, 2014).
2. Sugata Bose, *His Majesty's Opponent—Subhas Chandra Bose and India's Struggle against Empire*, (Gurgaon, Haryana, India: Penguin Books, 2013).
3. *Netaji Collected Works*, vol. 8: *India's Ambassador Abroad: Letters, Articles, Speeches and Statements 1933-1937*, Calcutta, 1994.
4. http://en.wikipedia.org/wiki/Tehran_Conference.
5. Wikipedia, *Modern Review*, December 27, 2014.
6. http://en.wikipedia.org/wiki/Chittagong_armoury_raid.
7. Eleven attachments, letters of the Polish diplomatic missions and central institutions, 1933-36.

COPY

Ref, no. 57/A/a/2   28th June 1933

Re: selling of Polish products

in India under British rule

Polish Institute of Export in Warsaw

The President of the Congress for Bengal who is currently in Vienna has visited the Embassy together with other Indian outstanding activists and showed vivid interest in Poland. He asked to be given exhaustive data as to the Polish products which could find demand in Eastern India especially in Calcutta where Mr. Bose was the Mayor of the City for a longer period of time.

Mr Subhas-Chandre Bose, his Secretary I. S. Mathur and Mr Widymski from the Austrian-Polish Chamber of Commerce attended a conference which took place in the Embassy.

During the discussion the gentlemen from India were given general information about the various branches in Polish industry. They are interested in importing to India products from the industry branches given below:

1/ cotton products

2/ artificial silk

3/ paper

4/ cement

5/ sugar

6/ paraffin, ozocerite and lubricating oil

7/ agricultural machines

8/ pipes for water lines and gas

9/ locomotives and train carriages

10/ narrow-gauge railroad

11/ railway tracks

12/ nails and screws

13/ enamelware

14/ spirits

15/ hop

Upon the Embassy's advice Mr. Bose probably with his Secretary will go to Warsaw in order to discuss the details needed to assess the possibility of selling the above mentioned products

Institute. Mr. Bose will leave tomorrow, i.e. the 29th June 1933 and will travel via Prague where he will probably stay for about 10 days so he would arrive in Warsaw around the 12th of July. The appropriate Polish economic unions would therefore have the time to prepare the required information for Mr. Bose.

On the other hand Mr. Bose is interested in the possibility of selling Eastern Indian products in Poland and through us he would like to address the competent parties in Poland to provide information and suggestions in this aspect.

Mr. Bose will have a letter to Director Turski or to his deputy in case Director Turski would not be in Warsaw in the middle of July.

As far as we know recently Consul Banasiński was to come to Poland from Bombay. If in the middle of July he would be in Warsaw then maybe there would be some possibility to allow him to meet Mr. Bose.

The Embassy only provides the above information and leaves it to the discretion of the State Export Institute to take further action.

Mr. Bose shall have with him letters of recommendation to the Chamber of Commerce and Industry in Warsaw and to the Central Union of Polish Industry, Commerce, Mining and Finance.

M. Mościcki
Chargé d'Affaires

Addressees:
P.II – Ministry of Foreign Affairs
P.III
Ministry of Industry and Commerce

odpis

Nr.57/A/a/2

28 czerwca 1933 r.

w spr.:zbytu towarów polskich
w Indjach angielskich.

Do Państwowego Instytutu Eksportowego

w Warszawie

Zgłosił się w Poselstwie bawiący obecnie w Wiedniu
wraz z innymi wybitnymi działaczami Indusów,prezes kongresu
na Bengalję p.Subhas C.Bose i dał wyraz swemu żywemu zaintere
sowaniu się Polską.Prosił on o dostarczenie mu możliwie wy-
czerpujących danych co do produktów polskich,któreby mogły
znaleźć zbyt w Indjach Wschodnich,zwłaszcza w Kalkucie,gdzie
p.Bose przez dłuższy czas sprawował funkcje prezydenta miasta.

Na konferencji,która odbyła się w Poselstwie,uczestni-
czył p.Subhas-Chandre Bose,jego sekretarz I.S.Mathur,oraz z
ramienia austrjacko-polskiej Izby Handlowej p.Widymski.

W dyskusji udzielono wymienionym panom z Indji informa-
cji ogólnych o stanie rozmaitych gałęzi polskiego przemysłu.
Chodzi im o zbadanie możliwości importu do Indji wyrobów na-
stępujących gałęzi przemysłu:

1/ Wyrobów bawełnianych
2/ sztucznego jedwabiu
3/ papieru
4/ cementu
5/ cukru
6/ parafiny,ozokerytu i olejów smarowych
7/ maszyn rolniczych
8/ rur dla wodociągów i przewodów gazowych
9/ lokomotyw i wagonów kolejowych
10/ kolejek wązkotorowych
11/ szyn kolejowych
12/ gwoździ i śrub
13/ naczyń emaljowanych
14/ spirytusu
15/ chmielu.

Za poradą Poselstwa wybiera się p.Bose,prawdopodobnie
w towarzystwie swego sekretarza do Warszawy,aby omówić za pośrednictwem Państwowego Instytutu Eksportowego z przedstawi-
cielami poszczególnych związków przemysłowych,szczegóły po-
trzebne do oceny możliwości zbytu wspomnianych wyżej produktów
w Indjach Wschodnich.Wyjazd p.Bose nastąpi jutro dnia 29 czerw
ca b.r.przez Pragę,gdzie p.Bose zatrzyma się prawdopodobnie
około 10 dni,tak iż przybyłby on do Warszawy około 12 lipca.
Związki gospodarcze tutaj w grę wchodzące miałyby więc czas
przygotować dla p.Bose potrzebny materjał.

Z drugiej strony interesuje się p.Bose możliwościami
zbytu w Polsce produktów Indyj Wschodnich i zwraca się za na-
szem pośrednictwem do kompetentnych czynników w Polsce o
udzielenie mu pod tym względem potrzebnych informacyj i wskazó
wek.

P.Bose wylegitymuje się pismem do p.Dyrektora Turskie-
go,względnie jego zastępcy,na wypadek,gdyby p.Dyrektor Turski
w połowie lipca nie był obecny w Warszawie.

O ile Poselstwu wiadomo,miał Konsul Banasiński przybyć
niedawno z Bombaju do Polski.W razie gdyby przebywał on w
połowie lipca w Warszawie,nadarzałaby się sposobność zetknię
cia go z p.Bose.

Poselstwo podaje powyższe do wiadomości,pozostawiając
uznaniu Państwowego Instytutu Eksportowego dalsze traktowa-
nie tej sprawy.

P.Bose otrzymuje również listy polecające do Izby
Przemysłowo-Handlowej w Warszawie i do Centralnego Związku
Polskiego Przemysłu,Handlu,Górnictwa i Finansów.

                          /-/M.Mościcki
                          Chargé d'Affaires

otrzym:

P.11 - MSZ
P.111   "
Min.Przem.i H.

Consulate of Poland   1st July 1936

in Bombay   COPY

351-a/1

Association of Friends of India

<u>Addressee:</u>

Ministry of Foreign Affairs P.VI.

The Embassy of the Republic of Poland in London

The Consulate of Poland is sending to your attention information given in the nationalistic press published by the Indian press agency "United Press" which concern the establishment of the "Society of Friends of India".

Eugeniusz Banasiński, Ph. D

Consul of the Republic of Poland

To:

Ministry of Foreign Affairs

Department P.III.

Warsaw

Rzeczypospolitej Polskiej
w R O M B A I U

351-a/1.   ODPIS

Towarzystwa Przyjaciół Indyj.
————————————————————————————
zielnik:
————————————
Z.P.VI.
sada RP.
ondynie.
ł.
——

> Ambasada Rzplt.P. w Londynie
>   6 - AUG.1936?
> No. 3 57 - ŻA——— 17

        Konsulat R.P. przesyła do wiadomości
informację podaną w tutejszej prasie nacjo-
nalistycznej przez indyjską agencję prasową
"United Press", dotyczącą założenia w Warszawie "Towarzystwa Przyjaciół Indyj.-

                    Dr. Eugenjusz Banasiński
                      Konsul R P.

Do

Ministerstwa Spraw Zagranicznych,
Wydział P.III.,

        W a r s z a w a.
        ————————————————

THE BOMBAY SENTINEL, SATURDAY, JU

Indian Museum In Warsaw

Indo-Polish Society Seeks To Bring Culture Of 2 Countries Nearer

WARSAW, June 15.
(By Air Mail).

Friends of India and lovers of Indian culture have recently founded a society under the two-fold name of "Bharata-Mitra-Parishad" in Sanskrit and (take a deep breath) "Towarzystwo Przyjacio Indji" in Polish.

As is evident from the title and as set down in the Constitution of the society, membership is only open to all persons of Polish and Indian nationality without any distinction of caste or creed

PRINCIPAL AIM

In fact the principal aim of the Bharata-Mitra Parishad is to propagate and popularize knowledge of India in Poland with a view to promoting closer relations between the two countries, by an exchange of ideas and intelligence, cultural and commercial, not barring, however, such information of current events as would undoubtedly be required to make any contact with India a real one.

PROPOSED BRANCHES

The society has its premises in Warsaw at present, but it aspires to open branches in all cultural centres of Poland in the near future. The proposed activities of the society can be summarised as follows:—

Disseminating Culture

1. Organising public meetings, conferences and lectures on real as well as historical India, by specialists on Indian matters.

2. Establishing libraries and reading rooms specially devoted to India in principal towns of Poland.

3. Opening local branches of the society in all principal towns of the country.

4. Generally giving assistance to Indian visitors to Poland, and specially encouraging Indian students to come to Poland for under-graduate as well as post-graduate studies, and facilitating the stay of such students.

In view of the above, the society is divided into three sections, viz., (1) Cultural, (2) Economic and commercial and (3) academic.

1. Cultural section has for its purpose the holding of public lectures and conferences, etc., by Indologists and other specialists on academic as well as living subjects. It will also be instrumental in bringing Polish and Indian savants into a closer contact.

Primary Task

2. The primary task of the Economic and Commercial section is to collect materials for and prepare statistics and other records of existing commercial relations between the two countries as well as to consider the possibilities of a further development of those relations. In this the society has the promise of the collaboration of several Polish economists and representatives of various official and private organizations.

3. The organisers of the society pay particular attention to the third section, viz., the Academic one whose object is to encourage Indian students to come to Po-

land. All information regarding the Polish school and university education will be furnished by the society in the form of a pamphlet which will be despatched to all Indian universities and students' societies. Also this section will take upon itself the task of procuring free board and lodging to Indian students and eventually scholarships and stipends for studying in Poland. In this, the society has the assurance of help from the official authorities.

Honorary Members

Apart from ordinary members, honorary members will be selected from those persons in Poland and India, who have rendered some service to the cause of bringing the two countries closer to each other.

Among the principal organisers of the Bharata-Mitra-Parisad may be mentioned the names of Professor Dr. Stanisaw Schayer, the president of the society, an eminent Indologist (well-known to readers of "Prabuddha Bharata") and head of the Oriental Institute of the Warsaw University of Joseph Pisudski, Mr. Shavlovski a former acting consul in Bombay and Mr. Hiranmoy Ghoshal, lecturer in Modern Indian languages and literatures at the Warsaw University of Joseph Pisudski.

Indian Museum

The Bharata-Mitra-Parisad has in view the formation of an Indian Museum in Warsaw for which purpose it has already received the kind permission of using the premises of the Warsaw Oriental Institute from Prof. Dr. Schayer. The Society will very soon issue a general appeal to the public in India and particularly to those kind friends who would be willing to contribute to the organization of such a mu-

The Embassy of Poland in Vienna   Vienna, 11th August 1934

Commercial Attache   CONFIDENTIAL

Re: actions of Mr. S.C. Bose- the former

Mayor of Calcutta regarding the

Indian-Central European Society in Vienna

Ministry of Foreign Affairs

P.III.

in Warsaw

In reference to the letter of the Ministry of 12.06.1934 ref. no. P.III.352 I-A/1 the Embassy communicates the following:

Foremost the Embassy refers to its letter to the Ministry of 28.06.1934 ref. no. 57A-a-2 directed to the Polish Institute of Export and for the attention of the Ministry of Foreign Affairs on the conferences that took place in our Embassy with Mr. Bose and his visit in Warsaw which was our initiative.

The Embassy is attaching a copy of this letter and informs that Mr. Bose and people in his closest surroundings still keep in touch with us.

The Association "Indian Central European Society" established by him functions on the charters written in German which I am sending as an attachment to this report. It is worthwhile noticing that art.1 provides an option for the Association's activity not only in Austria but also abroad by establishing its branches outside of Vienna, especially in main capital cities of Central Europe and India. Apart from electing Mr. Bose (staying in Vienna for a few months) as the president, Mr. Jagdish Singh Mathur and Mr. Nand Gairola – Indians who leave in Vienna were also elected to the Management Board of the Association. From the Austrian side the following people were elected to the Management Board: former Minister - Kolei Pesta, Otton Faltis – President of the "Oesterreichische Escomptverband", advisor to the minister in the Austrian Ministry of Trade – Teodor Sawicki Ph. D., Leopold Bermann – Professor in the Vienna Trade Academy and a few other people. Mr. Faltis was elected as the Vice-president and will run the office of the Association which is in Vienna at Tuchlauben 7a. The Association is only starting its activity. From the words of Mr. Bose and his companions it should be assumed that he and his organization are vividly interested in establishing relations between Poland and India. Mr. Faltis has already prepared a draft of two chapters of the branch organization namely the Indian Central European Society for Poland. This Society according to the author, would only be very generally associated with the Vienna organization, i.e. persons from the Vienna organization would assist in creation of its Polish chapter. The development of economic relations between Poland and India would be conducted by direct contacts between the two countries.

Our Embassy has suggested that the Eastern Institute together with the Union of Chambers of Commerce in Warsaw could take action in creating the above mentioned organization.

Mr. Bose and his organization are now awaiting specific proposals from the Polish side.

Regarding the above the Embassy would like to point out that another organisation established by the Indians exists in Vienna, i.e. "Austro-Indian Society" where Mr. Pundit Agnihotri permanently residing in Vienna is the President. The latter association is more of a social club and has its meetings on the premises of the local Kulturbund. There is a strong antagonism between Mr. Bose's and Mr. Agnihotri's association. Bose supports the independence, however one can think that his radicalism towards England is not as extreme as before. Agnihotri supports an agreement with England. He is currently carrying out propaganda aimed at organizing a trip to India for research and economic purposes. Mr. Bose and people very close to him are disrespectful towards Agnihotri's activities and in this way making it clear that they consider him as a paid agent of the English.

For some time Vienna has become a gathering point for the Indians coming to Central Europe. Vienna owes its attractiveness most of all to the local doctors and health sanatoriums. The Viennese medical school has become very famous in India. Moreover, there are many young Indian people in Vienna who study various faculties. According to the attached circular of the Indian Central-European Society Mr. Bose has moved the office of the Federation of Indian Students Abroad from London to Vienna.

4 attachments

Addressees:

Ministry of Foreign Affairs – P.III

Polish Export Institute

The Embassy of the Republic of Poland in London

S. Lalicki

Commercial Attache

Hdot.

POSELSTWO
RZECZYPOSPOLITEJ POLSKIEJ Z
W WIEDNIU

RADCA HANDLOWY

W SPRAWIE akcji S.C.Bose
b.mera miasta Kalkutty, wzgl.
Indo-środkowo-europejskiego
T-wa na terenie Wiednia
NR. 352/tj/A/1

Wiedeń, dnia 11 sierpnia 1934r.

Poufne

Do

Ministerstwa Spraw Zagranicznych

P.III.

w Warszawie

Odnośnie do pisma Ministerstwa z 12.VI.br.Nr.P.III.352
I-A/1, Poselstwo komunikuje,co następuje:

Przedewszystkiem Poselstwo powołuje się na pismo swe
do Ministerstwa z 28.VI.br.Nr.57A/a/2, skierowane do PIE, a
udzielone do wiadomości Ministerstwu Spraw Zagranicznych z o-
kazji konferencyj, odbytych z p.Bose w tut.Poselstwie i wyjaz-
du jego do Warszawy,przedsięwziętego za naszą inicjatywą.

Załączając kopję tego pisma,Poselstwo donosi,że p.Bo-
se i osoby,należące do jego bliższego otoczenia nadal utrzy-
mują kontakt z Poselstwem.

Założone przez niego Stowarzyszenie "Indian Central
European Society" opiera się na statutach,których tekst w ję-
zyku niemieckim załącza się do niniejszego raportu.Na uwagę
zasługuje przewidziana w par.1 działalność tego Stowarzyszenia nietylko w Austrji,lecz także i zagranicą, a tó przez u-
tworzenie filjalnych organizacyj poza Wiedniem,zwłaszcza w
głównych stolicach Europy Środkowej i w Indjach.Do Zarządu
Stowarzyszenia wybrano prócz p.Bose,przebywającego od szeregu miesięcy w Wiedniu/,jako przewodniczącego,zamieszkałych tutaj hindusów:pp.Jagdish Singh Mathur i Nand Gairola, a z Aus-
trjaków:b.ministra Kolei Pesta, Ottona Faltisa,przewodniczące-
go instytucji "Oesterreichische Escompteverband", radcę min.
w austr.m-wie Handlu,Dra Teodora Sawickiego, Dra Leopolda
Bermanna,profesora Wied.Akademji Handlowej i kilka innych o-

22.

sób. P.Faltis wybrany został wiceprezesem,przyczem powierzo
no mu prowadzenie biura Stowarzyszenia,które mieści się w
Wiedniu I,Tuchlauben 7a.

Działalność Stowarzyszenia jest dopiero w zaczątkach.

Z wynurzeń p.Bose i jego otoczenia sądzićby należało,
że on i jego organizacja interesują się żywo sprawą nawiąza
nia stosunków między Polską a Indjami.P.Faltis opracował na
wet szkic dwóch pierwszych paragrafów Stowarzyszenia filjal
nego dla Polski /Indian Central-European Society for Poland
jak świadczy załącznik Nr.2/. To Stowarzyszenie miałoby według słów autora statutu tylko luźny związek ze stowarzysze
niem wiedeńskiem,polegający na tem,że osoby,które założyły
organizację wiedeńską, uczestniczyłyby w pracy nad utworze-
niem organizacji polsko-indyjskiej. Rozbudowa stosunków gos
podarczych między Polską a Indjami odbywałaby się drogą bez
pośredniego kontaktu między temi krajami.

Poselstwo wysunęło myśl,aby sprawą utworzenia wspomnia
nej organizacji w Polsce zajął się Instytut Wschodni z ewen
tualnym udziałem Związku Izb Handlowych w Warszawie.

P.Bose względnie jego stowarzyszenie oczekuje w powyż-
szej sprawie konkretnych propozycyj ze strony polskiej.

W związku z tem Poselstwo zauważa,iż istnieje w Wiedni
druga organizacja,założona przez Hindusów,a mianowicie "Austro-Indian Society",pod przewodnictwem stale w Wiedniu zami
szkałego p.Pundit Agnihotri.To ostatnie stowarzyszenie jest
więcej klubem towarzyskiem i zbiera się w lokalu tut.Kultur-
bundu.Między grupą p.Bose a grupą p.Agnihotriego istnieje
silny antagonizm.Bose stoi na gruncie niepodległościowym,
choć odnosi się wrażenie,że radykalizm jego w stosunku do
Anglji nie jest tak skrajny, jak dawniej. Agnihotri jest zwo-

31

lennikiem porozumienia z Anglją.Rozwija on obecnie propagan-
dę za zorganizowaniem podróży dla celów naukowych i gospodar
czych do Indji.Bose i jego najbliźsi wyrażają się o akcji
Agnihotriego lekceważąco:,dając do poznania,że uważają go
za płatnego ajenta Anglików.

Od pewnego czasu Wiedeń stał się punktem zbornym Hindusów,przybywających do Europy Środkowej.Atrakcję swoją za-
wdzięcza Wiedeń przedewszystkiem tutejszym lekarzom i sana-
torjom.Wiedeńska szkoła medyczna zdobyła sobie w Indjach o-
gromną sławę.Nadto przebywa w Wiedniu sporo młodych Hindusów
dla studjów w rozmaitych gałęziach.Według załączonego cyrku-
larza Indyjskiego Centr.Europ.T-wa, p.Bose przeniósł siedzi-
bę Związku "Federation of Indian Students Abroad" z Londynu
do Wiednia .

4 załączniki.

Rozdzilenik:
MSZ - P.II.
PIE
Ambasada R.P.Londyn

/ S.Lalicki /
Radca Handlowy

The Embassy of Poland in Vienna

Vienna, 20th October 1934

Commercial Attache

Re: Indian-Central European Society in Vienna

L.352/tj/A/2

Ministry of Foreign Affairs

P.III.

in Warsaw

The Indian Central-European Society (vide the report of our Embassy in Vienna of 11th August 1934 ref, no. 352/tj/A/1 as an answer to the letter from the Ministry of Foreign Affairs of 12th June 1934 ref. no. P.III.352/II-A/1) has asked The Embassy of Poland in Vienna for information if competent Polish partners (The Eastern Institute together with the Union of the Chambers of Commerce Union in Warsaw) have already made a decision to establish a similar Indo-Polish organization.

According to the information given by the Vice-President of the above mentioned Society to our Embassy it is conducting a great deal of activity in order to develop trade relations between Austria and Eastern India. (…)

6 dot

38

POSELSTWO
RZECZYPOSPOLITEJ POLSKIEJ
W WIEDNIU

WIEDEŃ, DNIA 20.października 4.
IV. ARGENTINIERSTRASSE 25—27

Radca Handlowy

W SPRAWIE indo-środkowo-europejskiego towarzystwa na terenie Wiednia.

ODP. NA PISMO Z DN. 195

NR.

MINISTERSTWO SPRAW Z.
No P.III.352/J.A/7.
WESZŁO 27 PAŹ 1934
załączn. 2

L.352/tj/A/2

Do

Ministerstwa Spraw Zagranicznych

P.III.

w Warszawie.
- - - - - - - - - - - - - - - - - - - -

Stowarzyszenie Indian Central-European Society
/ vide raport tut.Poselstwa z dnia 11.sierpnia 1934
Nro 352/tj/A/1 w odpowiedzi na pismo Ministerstwa Spraw
Zagranicznych z dnia 12.czerwca b.r. Nro P.III.352/I-
A/1 / zwróciło się do Poselstwa z prośbą o informację,
czy kompetentne czynniki polskie / Instytut Wschodni
z ewentualnym udziałem Związku Izb handlowych w Warszawie / zajęły już stanowisko co do utworzenia analo-
gicznej organizacji polsko-indyjskiej.

Według informacyj udzielonych Poselstwu przez
wiceprezesa wspomnianego na wstępie stowarzyszenia
rozwija ono żywą działalność w kierunku rozbudowy stosunków handlowych między Austrją i Indjami Wschodniemi
Praca ta polega głównie na korespondencji z organiza-

The Consulate of the Republic of Poland   Bombay, 16th May 1934

  in Bombay

Ref. no. 351-b/1/pf

Re: situation concerning S.C. Bose-

former Mayor of Calcutta   CONFIDENTIAL

answer to ....

dated...............................

attachments ....

The Reuters agency informs on the 3rd of May that there was a meeting in Vienna in the Vienna Chamber of Commerce where the Indo-Central European Association for commercial and cultural relations between India and Austria was established. Former minister Pest was presiding and Mr. Bose was also present. Mr. Bose is about to leave for Prague to establish a similar organization there. With reference to the above please kindly advise me on Mr. Bose's efforts to establish further contacts with us and at what stage is his initiative which was presented last year in the Eastern Institute regarding the establishment of the Indo-Polish Association.

The already established Austro-Indian association is said to have already started in its premises a permanent exhibition of Indian products and intends to organize the Indian pavilion at the autumn Vienna Fair with special emphasis on Indian agriculture and mineral raw materials.

The office of the association is at Parkring 8 in Vienna.

I think that in our current trade situation and business connections which the Consulate creates it would be appropriate to authorize the Eastern Institute to give Mr. Bose's concepts a real form, if he should make any attempts in establishing a Polish - Indian Association.

                                  E. Banasiński Ph.D

                                  The Consul

                                  of the Republic of Poland

To:

The Ministry of Foreign Affairs

P.III

Copy to The Embassy of the Republic of Poland in London

KONSULAT
RZECZYPOSPOLITEJ POLSKIEJ
W BOMBAJU

BOMBAJ, Dn. 16 maja 193 4 R.

Nr. 351-b/1/pf

P O U F N E

W sprawie akcji S.C.Bose

~~ex-mera~~ m.Kalkuty.

W odpowiedzi na Nr.

z dnia

Załączników

Według doniesień Reutera pod datą 3 maja z Wiednia, odbyło się w Wiedeńskiej Izbie Handlowej pod przewodnictwem ex-ministra Pesta przy udziale p.Bose zebranie, na którem utworzone zostałe indo-środkowo-europejskie towarzystwo dla celów handlowego i kulturalnego zbliżenia Indyj i Austrji.

P.Bose ma udać się z Wiednia do Pragi dla zorganizowania tam takiegoż towarzystwa.

W związku z powyższą akcją p.Bose chodziłoby mi o wyjaśnienie, czy p.Bose starał się o nawiązanie z nami dalszych kontaktów, i jak przedstawia się rzucona przez niego w r.u. w Instytucie Wschodnim myśl utworzenia towarzystwo polsko-indyjskiego.

Powstałe towarzystwo austrjacko-indyjskie zapoczątkkowało już jakoby w swym lokalu stałą wystawę produkcji indyjskiej i nosi się obecnie z zamiarem zorganizowania indyjskiego pawilonu na jesiennych Targach Wiedeńskich ze specjalnem uwzględnieniem działu, poświęconego surowcom indyjskim - roślinnym i mineralnym.

Lokal towarzystwa mieści się Parkring 8,Wien I.

Byłbym zdania, iż w obecnych naszych zaawansowaniach handlowych i powiązaniach, jakie stwarza Konsulat, byłoby wskazane, w razie jeśli p.Bose uczyni jakieś nowe awanse w kierunku zorganizowania towarzystwa polsko-indyjskiego upoważnić Instytut Wschodni do nadania jego koncepcji realnych form.

Dr.E.Banasiński
Konsul R.P.

Do

Ministerstwa Spraw Zagranicznych

P.III.

Odpis do Ambasady R.P. w Londynie.

Consulate

of the Republic of Poland

in Bombay

351-b/4

Situation concerning S.C. Bose

E/27185/3.d.

5th November 1934

22nd November 1934

STRICTLY CONFIDENTIAL

(...) We should bear in mind that the whole of India, no matter of what political direction, realizes how much their economic life is suppressed by the English policy of preferences and quasi protection. They will willingly see (there is also a political element in this) commercial proposals from other countries aimed at weakening the economic strength of England in India.

It is this element that in my opinion plays an essential role in the concepts of Mr. Bose as far as the economic matters are concerned.

Therefore I think that by creating a Polish-Indian economic and cultural association we can only win but never loose, especially when the action of Mr. Bose will find lively response in the self government economic institutions of India and when they will start co-operating in that activity. This co-operation, as I see it, would take shape of introducing economy of this or other country into the territory of India and to influence the mind of an Indian merchant and industrialist in order to seek relations without political conflicts. If however, Mr. Bose would treat his action in isolation from the real Indian life, then I think that the possible creation of the Polish-Indian association would bring no tangible economic advantages to both parties. In that situation one should treat the whole situation of the creation of the association as Mr. Bose's leading idea to which I referred to above.

Bearing this in mind I do not suppose that the possible Polish-Indian association could stand in contradiction and conflict with works of currently operating commercial network in India. On the contrary I think that it will be very helpful and especially if the proposals of Mr. Bose will find support in the self governing commercial entities of India. If during the future activities of the association, new forces would emerge, aiming at some practical commercial tasks, then I am convinced that there is sufficient volume of work to be done.

I even think that we should actively support and act towards such aims, as both the work of the Consulate and the existing business infrastructure, in spite of much efforts and work, is not capable to cover the region equivalent in size to Europe.

E. Banasiński Ph. D

Consul of the Republic of Poland

2 ard-

KONSULAT
Rzeczypospolitej Polskiej
w BOMBAJU
351-b/4
akcji p.Bose.

E/27185/3.D.
5 listopada 1934 r.

ODPIS

M S Z. Nr. dz. 352/Jud/10
Date 10/XII 34

22 listopada 4 50

SCISLE POUFNE

Odpowiadając na powyższe pismo w sprawie
działalności p.Bose,zarówno z czasu jego zamieszkiwania w Indjach,jak i jego obecnego pobytu w Europie,komunikuję:

Subash Chandra Bose,były "Chief Executive
Office of Calcutta Municipality",należy do najwybitniejszych
przedstawicieli ruchu niepodległościowego Indyj Bryt..Za cza-
sów swej działalności w Indjach uważany był nawet w sferach
kongresowych za nieprzejednanego ekstremistę.Bezwzględność,z
jaką pchał do walki,nawet czynnej,spowodowała wśród kongresis-
tów Bengalu,gdzie głównie występował,rozłam na dwa obozy - Subash Bose i Sen Gupta,które przetrwały do dziś dnia.- Dużo uwagi poświęcał ruchowi robotniczemu.W lipcu 1931 wystąpił,jako
przewodniczący 11-ej sesji związku robotniczego Kongresu w Kal-
kucie/Trade Union Congress/.- W czasie ostatniej akcji nieposłu
szeństwa cywilnego aresztowany został przez władze indyjskie
i osadzony w więzieniu,jako "State Prisoner"/więzień państwa/.
Wkrótce jednak został zwolniony z więzienia pod warunkiem opu-
szczenia Indyj.Pozostawił jednak mocną grupę swych zwolenników
w Bengalu,która do dziś uważana jest za grupę Chandra Bose w
odróżnieniu od grupy Sen Gupta,bardziej umiarkowanej w swej
taktyce politycznej.

Jeśli chodzi o teren europejski,to nie ule-
ga wątpliwości,iż przewodnią ideą akcji p.Bose jest jaknajszers
sze pozyskanie sympatji i moralnego poparcia opinji europejs-

Do

Państwowego Instytutu Eksportowego

w Warszawie.

351-b/4   22 listopada 1934 r.   II. 5/

kiej dla sprawy niepodległościowej Indyj i rzucenia ich na sze-
lę walki politycznej,prowadzonej w Indjach.

        O ile mi wiadomo,p.Bose w swej akcji nie ogra-
nicza się jedynie do terenu środkowo-europejskiego.W lecie od-
wiedził
Budapeszt a również Bukareszt,Sofję i Belgrad,gdzie spotkał się
jak wynika z jego rewelacyj prasowych,z bardzo serdecznem przy-
jęciem zarówno ze strony oficjalnych czynników,jak i prasy.
Mniej szczęśliwa była jego wizyta w Belgradzie.Tutaj,naskutek
interwencji posła angielskiego,jugosłowiańskie M.S.Z.wstrzyma-
ło opublikowanie jego wywiadu prasowego,co znalazło echo zarówno w enuncjacji Reutera,jak United Press/indyjska organizacja
prasowa/,prostującej nieścisłe informacje Reutera co do wstrzy-
mania przez władze jugosłowiańskie wywiadu p.Bose.

        Trudno mi sądzić,czy akcja p.Bose znajduje
oparcie w Kongresie,którego p.Bose był niegdyś filarem,czy też
może jedynie w niepodległościowych organizacjach Bengalu, z których wyrósł p.Bose.Jeśli nawet na razie nie jest ona związana
organicznie z ich wytycznemi pracy/gdy chodzi o zagranicę/,to
w każdym razie i w każdej chwili może ona liczyć na ich jaknaj-
bardziej życzliwe przyjęcie i poparcie.Trudno mi sądzić również
w jakim stopniu koncepcje gospodarcze p.Bose,zamknięte w ramacl
towarzystw środkowo-europejskich,znajdują dziś już swój odpowiednik w indyjskich izbach handlowych/należy odróżniać je od
izb handlowych,kierowanych przez anglików/.Udzielone mi na ten
temat wyjaśnienia przez wiceprezydenta indyjskiej izby handlowej w Bombaju p.Manu Suberdar wskazują,iż izba bombajska nie
jest na razie wciągnięta w akcję gospodarczego zbliżenia Indyj
i Kontynentu,prowadzoną przez p.Bose.P.Suberdar podkreślił jednak,iż w razie zwrócenia się p.Bose czy też organizacyj indo-
europejskich,powstałych za jego inicjatywą,o nawiązanie gospod:

351-b/4   22 listopada 1934 r.   III. 52

nich o spółdziałanie w tej akcji,izby niewątpliwie pójdą na-
spotkanie w jaknajszerszem znaczeniu.

          Należy mieć na uwadze,iż całe Indje,niezależ-
nie od kierunków politycznych,zdają sobie sprawę,jak dalece
krępuje ich życie gospodarcze narzucana im przez Anglję polity-
ka preferencyj i quasi-protekcyj,i chętnie/wchodzi tu w grę moment polityczny/widziałyby zaawansowania handlowe innych krajów
prowadzące do osłabienia prężności gospodarczej Anglji na terenie Indyj.I ten moment,jak mogę sądzić,odgrywa pierwszorzędne
znaczenie w koncepcjach p.Bose,jeśli chodzi o stronę gospodar-
czą jego akcji.

          I przeto tworząc towarzystwo polsko-indyjskie
o zadaniach gospodarczo-kulturalnych,uważam,iż możemy jedynie
wygrać a nigdy przegrać,a zwłaszcza wygrać wówczas,gdy akcja
p.Bose znajdzie swój żywy odpowiednik na terenie indyjskich
gospodarczych instytucyj samorządowych i gdy one przyjmą na
siebie rolę spółdziałania w tej akcji na tutejszym terenie.
Spółdziałanie to,jak sobie wyobrażam,sprowadzałoby się do pro-
pagowania i wprowadzania terenu gospodarczego tego lub innego
kraju na teren Indyj i do oddziaływania na psychikę kupca i
przemysłowca indyjskiego w kierunku szukania związku tam,gdzie
nie wchodzi w grę konflikt polityczny.Gdyby jednak p.Bose trak-
tował swoją akcję w oderwaniu od bezpośredniości życia Indyj,
to nie wydaje mi się,ażeby ewent.powstałe towarzystwo polsko-
indyjskie mogło przynieść jakieś widoczne korzyści gospodarcze-
mu zbliżeniu stron.Wówczas należałoby traktować całą sprawę
towarzystwa pod kątem widzenia przewodniej idei p.Bose,do której nawiązuję wyżej.

          Na tle powyższego nie wydaje mi się,ażeby ak-
cja ewent.powstałego towarzystwa polsko-indyjskiego w tem lub

351-b/4   22   listopada   1934 r.   IV.
                                                    53

innem jej ujęciu mogła kolidować z pracami obecnie działają-
cego aparatu handlowego w Indjach.Przeciwnie,uważam,iż będzie
ona mu pomocną,a zwłaszcza,gdy ideę p.Bose znajdą poważne opa
rcie o indyjskie samorządowe aparaty handlowe.Gdyby jednak z
czasem wyłoniły się z łona towarzystwa nowe siły czy też nowe związki,zmierzające do zadań praktyczno-handlowych,to wydaje mi się,iż znajdą one w Indjach zawsze teren do pracy.
Sądziłbym nawet,iż winniśmy w tym kierunku zmierzać,gdyż zarówno akcja handlowa Konsulatu,jak i istniejącego aparatu
handlowego,mimo dużych wysiłków i pracy,nie jest w stanie
ogarnąć terenu równającego się pod względem wielkości Europie

                                        Dr.E.Banasiński
                                        Konsul R.P.

Odpis do wiadomości:
M.S.Z. P.III.
Ambasada R.P.w Londynie.   (...)

CONFIDENTIAL   6th August 1934

The Eastern Institute

Warsaw, Miodowa 7

Tel. 202-29 Head secretarial office

    522-21 operator

Ref. no. 113-34r.

Department for the East

at the Ministry of Foreign Affairs

Answering to the letter ref no. P.III.352/I-A/1 of 12. 06.1934 I would like to inform that the matter of the Polish-Indian Society has been in a dead point since the time of the visit of the ex – mayor of Calcutta, Subhas Chandra Bose, the reason being that he did not fulfill his promise of returning to Warsaw. In effect the initiative presented, was waiting for the promised return in few weeks or two months. Additionally other supporting voices in the matter, for example from Mr. St .Hulanicki, did not seem to sound serious enough.

The Eastern Institute did not so far undertake any action to organize such a society. This would require first of all some promotion, communication with Professor Stasiak in Lvov, Professor Willman Grabowska in Krakow, etc. Of course we can organize it in two or three weeks if only the Ministry of Foreign Affairs will approve this initiative which at the moment is not pursued. In this case it would be reasonable to appoint the president etc. in advance and then I could arrange a meeting on behalf of the Eastern Institute to establish such an association. I think that the best time to establish this association would be the second half of September. From the meeting which took place during Mr. Bose's visit I am giving you for your information a list of people who expressed their interest in joining the said association in the future.

                                  Prof. Olgierd Górka

                       Secretary General of the Eastern Institute

INSTYTUT WSCHODNI   P o u f n e   DNIA 6 sierpnia 1934r.

WARSZAWA, MIODOWA 7

TEL. 592-29 SEKR. GEN.
592-91 OGÓLNY

№113-34r.

Do

Ministerstwa Spraw Zagranicznych

Wydział Wschodni

w/m

W odpowiedzi na pismo P. III.352/I - A/1 z 12-VI br., pozwałam sobie poinfromować, że sprawa założenia Towarzystwa Polsko-Indyjskiego stanęła na martwym punkcie od czasu pobytu w Polsce b. mera Kalkuty Subhas Chandra Bose, a to z powodu niezrealizowanego jego zapewnienia, powrotu do Warszawy. W rezultacie rzucona wówczas inicjatywa zczekała na relizację do zapowiedzianego powrotu w ciągu kilku tygodni czy dwóch miesięcy. Pozatem, inne zapędy w tej sprawie np. p. St.Hulanickiego nie wydawały się dość poważne.

Instytut więc Wschodni nie podejmował akcji realizacji przynajmniej jak narazie, powołanie bowiem takiego Towarzystwa wymagałoby przedewszystkiem pewnej agitacji, porozumienia się np. z Profesorem

Stasiakiem we Lwowie, prof. Willman Grabowską w Krakowie i td. Oczywiście sprawa jest do zrealizowania w ciągu dwóch do trzech tygodni, o ile tylko M.S.Z. uważa za wskazane podjęcie inicjatywy chwilowo nie rozwijanej. W tym wypadku, wskazane byłoby ustalenie zgóry osoby prezesa i td., a wówczas z ramienia Instytutu Wschodniego zaaranżowałbym zebranie dla powołania do życia podobnego towarzystwa. Za okres czasu na podobne akcje nadający się uważam najwcześniej drugą połowę w rześnia. Dla orjentacji zebrania które miało miejsce swego czasu z okazji pobytu p. Bose, podaję spis osób, które zgłosiły wówczas swą chęć przystąpienia w przyszłości do podobnego Towarzystwa.

1 zał.

/Prof.Dr.Olgierd Górka/
Sekretarz generalny. I.W.

I I ATTACHMENTS

10th August 1934

Eastern Political-Economic

P.III.352/1-A/4

situation concerning S.C.Bose

In connection with the letter from the Consulate of 16th May 1934 ref. no. 351-b/1/pfn regarding the situation concerning Mr. S.C. Bose, the former Mayor of Calcutta, the Ministry of Foreign Affairs is sending to the attention as an attachment the copy of the letter from the Eastern Institute of 6th May ref. no. 113/34.

At the same time the Ministry would like to communicate that the subject of organizing the Polish-Indian Society will be considered in the case when the Indian side and Mr. Bose will approach us again.

Vice director

of the Political Department

pp. Jan Wszelaki

To: The Consulate of the Republic of Poland in Bombay

sierpnia 4

Polityczno-Ekonomiczny
Wschodni

P.III.352/1-A/4
akcji S.C.Bose

1

W związku z pismem Konsulatu z dnia 16
maja b.r.Nr.351-b/1/pfn.w sprawie akcji S.C.Bose
ex-mera Kalkuty,Ministerstwo Spraw Zagranicznych
przesyła w załączeniu odpis pisma Instytutu Wschc
dniego z dn.6 b.m.Nr.113/34 - do wiadomości.

Jednocześnie Ministerstwo komunikuje,że
sprawa organizowania T-wa Polsko-Indyjskiego będzie konkretnie rozpatrywaną w razie ponownego
jej podjęcia przez stronę indyjską,ew.przez p.
Bose.

Wicedyrektor
Departamentu Politycznego
w/z

/Jan Wszelaki/

Do
Konsulatu R.P.
w Bombaju

I I ATTACHMENTS

POLISH INSTUTUTE OF EXPORT

Ref. no. E/27034/3.D.   Warsaw, 31st October 1934

Re: ....

Department for the East
at the Ministry of Foreign Affairs

With reference to report of the Polish Embassy in Vienna of 20th May ref. no. 353/tj/A/2 and earlier correspondence about the Indian institutions in Austria and their interest in Polish-Indian economic relations-the Polish Institute of Export advises to exercise great caution while dealing with these matters. The Institute does not rule out that Mr. Bose's and Pundit Agnihotri's initiatives can be of an advantage to us. However, they can be in conflict with the activities of our own companies in India, i.e. the representation of "The Polish Industries Agency".

The Institute suggests that this case be analyzed in detail by the Consulate of the Republic of Poland in Bombay.

Director

M. Turski

Zdób.

PAŃSTWOWY INSTYTUT EKSPORTOWY

M. P. I H.

L. dz. E/27034/3.D.

W SPRAWIE

WARSZAWA. DN. 31 października 1934.
ELEKTORALNA 2.

Do

MINISTERSTWA SPRAW ZAGRANICZNYCH
Wydział Wschodni
w miejscu.
=========================

      Nawiązując do raportu Poselstwa R.P.
w Wiedniu z dnia 20 b.m. Nr.353/tj/A/2, oraz poprzedniej
korespondencji w sprawie instytucyj hinduskich w Austrji
i ich tendencyj do zainteresowania się stosunkami gospo-
darczemi polsko-indyjskiemi - Państwowy Instytut Eksportowy zauważa, że do spraw tych należałoby się odnosić z dużą
ostrożnością. Instytut nie wyklucza bynajmniej, że inicjatywy pp.Bose i Pundit Agnihotri mogą się okazać dla nas
korzystne - mogą one jednak stanąć w pewnej kolizji z dzia-
łaniem naszych własnych firm handlowych, pracujących z Indjami, a więc przedewszystkiem firmy "The Polish Industries
Agency".-

      Instytut proponuje, aby sprawę tę zbadał
szczegółowo Konsulat R.P. w Bombaju.-

Pro domo:

Gut/J.

D Y R E K T O R :

M.Turski

POLISH INSTUTUTE OF EXPORT

Ref. no. E/32020/3.D.   Warsaw, 18th December 1934

Re:

Department for the East
at the Ministry of Foreign Affairs

In reference to the letter of 13th December ref. no. P.III.352/I.A./10 the Polish Institute of Export is of the opinion that the proposed by Mr. Bose, Polish-Indian organization may indeed have positive influence on our economic relations with India and the Institute will gladly co-operate with such organization. However, we think that such organization should rather have general goals, i.e. cultural, political, etc and so should be established by a similar Polish institution. Our Institute is of the opinion that the Eastern Institute should organize the said society just as it had been suggested by the Ministry of Foreign Affairs in its letter of 30th October 1934 ref. no. P.III.352/JA/7. Explanations in the letter from the Consulate of the Republic of Poland support the Institute's opinion in regards to the above.

Director

M. Turski

10 dot.

54

PAŃSTWOWY INSTYTUT EKSPORTOWY

M. P. I H.

L. dz. E/32020/3.D.

W SPRAWIE ....

M. S. Z.
P III.

WARSZAWA, DN. 18 grudnia 1934 r.
ELEKTORALNA 2.

D o

MINISTERSTWA SPRAW ZAGRANICZNYCH
Wydział Wschodni

w   m i e j s c u
=========================

Nawiązując do pisma z dnia 13 b.m. Nr.
P.III.352/I.A./10, Państwowy Instytut Eksportowy stwierdza, iż
organizacja polsko-indyjska, proponowana przez p.Bose, mogła-
by istotnie oddziaływać dodatnio na nasze stosunki gospodarcze
z Indjami i w tym zakresie Instytut z organizacją taką współ-
pracowałby chętnie. Jednakowoż wydaje się, że organizacja taka
postawić sobie winna cele ogólne, a więc kulturalne, politycz-
ne et.c., a co za tem idzie, utworzona być winna pod egidą instytucji polskiej o podobnie szerokich zainteresowaniach. Z
tego względu Instytut uważa, iż sprawą tą należałoby zainte-
resować Instytut Wschodni, jak to Ministerstwo proponowało w
piśmie swem z dn.3o.października r.b. Nr.P.III.352/JA/7. Wyjaśnienia zawarte w piśmie Konsulatu R.P. w Bombaju umacniają
Instytut w poglądzie powyższym.

D Y R E K T O R :

M. Turski

The Embassy   Chungking, 22nd August

of the Republic of Poland

in Chungking

Re: remarks on the political deadlock in India

[Translator's remark: under the date there is a stamp stating the date the letter was delivered to the Ministry of Foreign Affairs, i.e. 7.09.1944]

Ministry of Foreign Affairs in London

(...) I take the liberty to submit to you Mr. Minister, in this communication a number of my own observations on the essential changes taking place in India. My opinions are derived practically exclusively from discussions with people taking direct part in shaping the present picture of India as well as on my own subjective impressions, after my few months of visiting such distant places like Calcutta, Madras, Bombay, Delhi and also the last year visit to Karachi."

British or other authors, whose equally subjective opinions are usually considered to be objective information material, in most cases got acquainted with one or two of the above centers as tourists and were lacking local contacts which I managed to find along the whole route.

That is why I feel encouraged to put forward opinions significantly differing from common publications in the British and other Allies press.

While preparing this report my main idea was to give to the Ministry comments on the phenomena in the Indian politics and Indo-British relations, which are not understood by the common continental mind, even more that the available literature on the subject is either questionable or extremely partisan due to the priori attitude of the authors.

It is a fact that this very significant problem of the future is being presented to the United Nations in a false manner of concepts and ideas not taking into account in a sufficient way the Indian reality which only few Britons managed to comprehend.

I suppose that as an ally of Great Britain we should avoid repeating in the subject of the future of the British Empire, light and trivial approaches and that it is necessary that our official sources should have elements enabling understanding a very complex policy of our British ally in this respect, which as a conclusion should be of assistance in the current diplomatic co-operation between Poland and Britain.

If we can show understanding of the India problems better than other allies, we shall gain greatly as a Government and in the area of diplomacy in the evaluations of the responsible British authorities. We cannot disregard possible practical benefits which this will give us in the period of setting new world order after defeating the totalitarian forces of the Axis.

Our own lightheartedness, ill located sentimentalism, alien suggestions, permanently coming from anti-British sources and the partisan British and Indian literature on Indian matters, have continuous influence on the shaping of Polish public opinion and cause statements which cannot be compatible with our or British basic interest.

reacting to seemingly small Polish mistakes ,offences and nuance, in India as well as on the platform of theoretical statements.

Letting the Poles come to India was an act of exceptional trust in us from the central British authorities and what is more important from the British authorities in India, with their influence on the great Imperial politics which is permanent and direct in contrast to the changing attitudes of London offices.

I take the liberty of posing the question if we realize this sufficiently and whether our Government offices deciding upon current refugee, administrative and personal matters, etc. take this into consideration at all. India is not some kind of Cyprus or Kenya where words of criticism or light remarks of guests from abroad on local relations, administration etc. are passed without comments, as these things are really of no care to the English.

If already today the administration of India exerts great influence upon the imperial politics as a whole then tomorrow after the establishment of a real self rule or few ambitious self ruling governments always tied with Great Britain with knots of defense, commerce and currency, that role will be much bigger and we will be sorry that we could not make use of the possibilities the war gave us to strengthen the positive attitudes and opinions on Poland necessary for developing economic co-operation etc. (…)

Alfred Poniński

The Ambassador of the Republic of Poland

AMBASADA
RZECZYPOSPOLITEJ POLSKIEJ
W CZUNGKINGU
Nr. Ch 3. 13, 44

Czungking, dnia 22 sierpnia
44

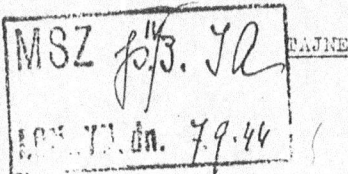

W sprawie: Uwagi, dotyczą-
ce deadlock'u politycznego
w Indiach.
- - - - - - - - - - - - - - - - -

MSZ fo 3. JR TAJNE

dn. 7.9.44

Do

Pana Ministra Spraw Zagranicznych

w L o n d y n i e
- - - - - - - - - - - - - - - - - - - -

D VII
P IV
P V } do wiad.

7.9.44 M

        Upływa już IV-ty miesiąc od chwili zwolnienia Gandhiego z
więzienia, które według oficjalnej tezy administracji brytyjskiej
nastąpiło wyłącznie ze względu na zagrożony stan jego zdrowia, ni
zaś celem podjęcia przy jego udziale generalnej próby wyjścia z
pasu tzw. "deadlock'u" politycznego w Indiach.

        Gorączkowa działalność, rozwijana przez Gandhiego w ciągu
ostatnich trzech miesięcy, w kierunku uchwycenia inicjatywy poli
nej w swoje ręce wskazywałaby na to, że stan jego zdrowia nie by
momencie zwolnienia tak niepokojący, jak to wszystkie zaintereso
czynniki brytyjskie i tubylcze starały się przedstawić.

        Niemniej wypada stwierdzić, że Wicekról wykazywał dotąd maks
ną rezerwę wobec różnych pojednawczych ofert i sugestii Gandhieg
którego wysiłki miały przede wszystkim na celu ponowne wprowadzeni
na arenę życia politycznego Indii Partii Kongresowej, której wsz
niemal przywódcy są dotąd pozbawieni wolności i której organizac
ulegla podczas tej wojny zewnętrznemu rozbiciu i /jak twierdzą p
stawiciele innych grup politycznych/ dość poważnemu wewnętrznemu
kładowi.

        Obecnie strona hinduska, oszczędzająca doniedawna Lorda Wave
wystąpiła przeciw niemu z zarzutem, że "zakochany jest w deadloc
politycznym i nie zamierza ułatwić prób jego likwidacji". Właści
sens tego oskarżenia jest szerszy: chodzi o stwierdzenie wobec o
demokratycznej całego świata, że rząd brytyjski nie chce odwołać
w końowej fazie wojny do pomocy i poparcia społeczeństwa hindus
go, które wyraża pełną w tym kierunku gotowość i gdyby mu tylko
pozwolono, mogłoby się przyczynić do szybszego zwycięstwa.

        Intencja takiego postawienia sprawy jest przejrzysta i nie
komentarzy. Nacjonalistyczna propaganda indyjska wychodzi z zalo
że ubezwłasnowolniona grupa polityków kongresowych i jej zdezorganizo
aparat identyczne są z całą społecznością tubylczą i. że wykazywa
przez administrację brytyjską niechęć zawarcia z nią nowego obec
          paktu czy kompromisu jest równoznaczne z odrzuceniem ud
łu indyjskiego w wspólnym wywalczeniu zwycięstwa Zjednoczonych N
dów, którego urzeczywistnienia masy indyjskie wszakże najgoręcej
pragną, identyfikując w nim realizację swych nadziei niepodległo
wych.

        Z powyższego wynika, że zasadnicza rozgrywka wpływów polity
na terenie Indii weszła w nową zupełnie fazę, w której wczorajsi
botażyści zwycięstwa Wielkiej Brytanii i organizowanego przez ni
brzymiego wysiłku wojennego Indii pragną się wykazać jako faktyc

(1)

3

lub tylko intencjonalni tych osiągnięć poplecznicy.

Administracja brytyjska natomiast obstaje twardo przy tym, aby odpowiedzialności winnych nie zostały teraz, w końcowym okresie wojny zatarte, licząc na to, że sama społeczność indyjska w takim wypadku wyciągnie wobec skompromitowanych polityków, którzy na początku wojny postawili na fałszywego konia, odpowiednie konsekwencje.

Pozwalam sobie przedłożyć Panu Ministrowi przy niniejszym zestawieniu szeregu syntetycznych obserwacji własnych, dotyczących dokonywujących się zasadniczych przemian w Indiach. Opinie moje opierają się niemal wyłącznie na wymianie zdań z ludźmi, biorącymi bezpośredni udział w kształtc aniu współczesnego oblicza Indii oraz na subjekt;wnych wrażeniach, wyniesionych z parumiesięcznej podróży, której s trasa obejmowała tak odległe od siebie centra, jak Kalkuta, Madras, Bombaj i Delhi /plus zeszłoroczne wrażenia z Karachi/.

Autorzy brytyjscy czy inni, których niemniej subjektywne tezy traktowane są zazwyczaj, jako objektywny materiał informacyjno-orientacyjny, poznali przeważnie powierzchownie i raczej w charakterze turystów jeden lub dwa z wymienionych ośrodków i pozbawieni byli tej ilości tubylczych kontaktów, jakie udało mi się na całej tej trasie nawiązać.

To właśnie ośmiela mnie do formułowania opinii, odbiegających bardzo znacznie od popularnych naogół tez, obiegających prasę brytyjską i aliancką.

Przy sporządzaniu tego opracowania przyświecała mi przede wszystkim myśl dania Ministerstwu komentarza do zjawisk w polityce indyjskiej i stosunków indyjsko-brytyjskich, które są dla przeciętnego umysłu kontynentalnego zgoła niezrozumiałe, a to tym bardziej, że dostępna na ten temat literatura jest albo polemiczna, albo wybitnie tendencyjna wskutek apriorystycznego nastawienia autorów. Faktem jest, że ten kapitalny problem przyszłości ukazuje się noraz Zjednoczonym Narodom w krzywym zwierciadle tez i hipotez, nie liczących się w dostatecznej mierze z rzeczywistością indyjską, którą... Brytyjczyków prawdziwie wzgłębiło. ... zagadnień komu...

Wydaje mi się, że jako alianci Wielkiej Brytanii powinniśmy uniknąć powtarzania w tej kwestii, dotyczącej jutra Imperium Brytyjskiego, banałów i że wskazanym jest, aby nasze urzędowe czynniki znalazły się w posiadaniu elementów, ułatwiających zrozumienie bardzo wycieniowanej polityki brytyjskiego alianta na tym odcinku, co powinno ułatwić w końcowym wywodzie bieżącą współpracę dyplomatyczną polsko-brytyjską.

Jeśli wykażemy lepsze od innych aliantów zrozumienie problematu Indii, zyskamy ogromnie jako Rząd i dyplomacja w opinii odpowiedzialnych sfer brytyjskich.

Niepodobna lekceważyć ewentualnych praktycznych korzyści, jakie by to nam dać mogło w okresie kształtowania się nowego świata porządku po rozgromieniu totalitarnych potęg Osi.

Własną lekkomyślność, źle umieszczony sentymentalizm, sugestia obca, płynąca stale ze źródeł antybrytyjskich, lub wreszcie tendencyjna literatura angielska i indyjska o sprawach Indii wpływają stale na kształtowanie się polskiej opinii i wypowiedzi w tym względzie, nie dających się pogodzić ani z naszą, ani też z brytyjską racją stanu.

- 3 -

Wynikającemu stąd złu nikt się dotąd nie przeciwstawia. Placówka nasza w Indiach była dotąd upośledzoną komórką administracyjną, organicznie niezdolną do zapoczątkowania jakiejś akcji w kierunku zwrócenia uwagi naszych czynników miarodajnych na ogromne konsekwencje bagatelizowania przez Rząd pozornie mało znaczących indywidualnych polskich błędów, poślizgnięć i nietaktów zarówno na terenie samych Indii, jak i na oderwanej płaszczyźnie teoretycznych wypowiedzi.

Wpuszczenie Polaków do Indii było aktem wyjątkowego zaufania dl nas ze strony centralnych władz angielskich i co ważniejsze, brytyjskich czynników w Indiach, których wpływ na wielką imperialną politykę brytyjską jest przecież stały i bezpośredni, w przeciwieństwie do zmiennego nastawienia większości poszczególnych biur londyńskich.

Pozwalam sobie postawić pytanie, czy uświadomiliśmy to sobie w dostatecznej mierze i czy nasz aparat rządowy, rozpatrując i decydując pewne bieżące sprawy uchodźcze, administracyjne, personalne i t.p., bierze to w ogóle pod uwagę. Indie, to nie jest jakiś Cypr czy Kenja, gdzie krytyki, czy lekceważące uwagi obcych gości na temat miejscowych stosunków, oblicza administracji i t.d. przemijają bez echa, bo w gruncie rzeczy są Anglikom zupełnie obojętne.

Jeżeli już dziś administracja Indii wywiera duży wpływ na politykę brytyjską w skali imperialnej, to jutro, po wytworzeniu się tam prawdziwego samorządu, lub paru ambitnych samodzielnych rządów, złączonych zawsze wspólnymi więzami obrony, handlu i pieniądza z Wielką Brytanią, rola ta będzie znacznie większa i wtedy będziemy żałować poniewczasie, że nie potrafiliśmy wykorzystać pomyślnej dla nas koniunktury wojennej dla ugruntowania tam dobrych dla Polski nastrojów i opinii, niezbędnych n.p. dla rozbudowy współpracy gospodarczej i t.p.

Jako pierwszą część opracowania załączam fragment, dotyczący stanowiska Gandhiego, roli przywódców kongresowych, taktyki brytyjskiej w okresie przejściowym i splotu zagadnień komunistyczno-wywrotowych. Dalsze fragmenty pozwolę sobie nadsyłać w miarę ich rozpracowania z powołaniem na niniejszy raport.

1 załącznik.

/Alfred Poniński/
AMBASADOR R.P.

AP/ZS

www.ingramcontent.com/pod-product-compliance
Lightning Source LLC
Chambersburg PA
CBHW021824270326
41932CB00007B/324